W9-AOI-605

This book is for

____

All my love,

____

You're the Best Mom Ever

You're the Best Mom Ever

Ellen Jacob

Andrews McMeel Publishing

Kansas City

 For information, write Andrews McMeel Publishing, an Andrews McMeel Universal company, 4520 Main Street, Kansas City, Missouri 64111.

01 02 03 04 05 RDC 10 9 8 7 6 5 4 3 2 1

ISBN: 0-7407-1159-8

Library of Congress Catalog Card Number: 00-108494

For my mom, whose support and wisdom
is the inspiration for this book, and
to Kirk, the love and joy of my life.

Acknowledging those who help in any project is always dubious at best. It is certain that someone important will be left out or that someone among the acknowledged ones will wish, in the end, that they had not been so publicly linked to something not their fault.

But in a book like this—a compilation of others' thoughts and feelings—acknowledgment almost seems redundant. The people who made this book are the people whose words follow—and they are all named.

Nonetheless, there are a few who really made this project what it is. Thanks to Laurin Sydney and Gail Evans, and Loretta Barrett, who independently embraced this project and introduced me to others who would do the same. Thanks to Jan Miller, who, without knowing it, started me on the path. And to Allan Stark, Tim Lynch, Kelly Gilbert, Julie Herren, Christi Clemons Hoffman, and the others at Andrews McMeel for their respect and help.

Thanks to my friend Leslie Singer, who has listened to me endlessly through many projects and always has an encouraging word and more than one creative idea. She also embraced this project, insisting she design the perfect cover—bold and feminine, just like her—a true expression of friendship. And to Cristina Lambert Clarke, for her insightful editing help. And to Kirk, without whose brilliance, support, and love, the punctuation would be wrong and I would be a ball of tears. Not a moment goes by that I am not grateful and exhilarated by your presence in my life. Thank you.

Ordinary Moments, Extraordinary Memories

Mom. There is a photo of mine sitting on my bookshelf. I took it while at art school. My mother, quite beautiful in black and white, with a wistful expression emerging from the dark shadow across her face. My mother is probably around the age I am now. We really look nothing alike, yet every now and then, if I walk quickly past the photo, I think I see myself. The old cliché is coming true: The older I get, the more I remind myself of my mother. This is a nice thing.

My mother always encouraged me to be the woman I wanted to be, not to conform to what the rest of my family was doing or what other women were becoming. My memories are numerous, made more vivid from speaking with everyone involved in this book. You will read them scattered throughout, along with others' memories, in the following pages.

As I interviewed people for this book—famous and not so famous, young and not so young, men and women—I was struck by how our most extraordinary memories often come from the ordinary moments. These are the moments that define our relationships with our moms and endure seemingly forever: the way our mothers brush their hair, or cook us breakfast, or call us when our relationships don't work out—these are the moments we have the most intimate feelings for Mom.

So I have gathered together ordinary and a few not so ordinary memories of Mom. This book is a tribute to moms everywhere, and in particular to one very special mother, my mom. You are all the best moms ever.

Our
Moms
Are Our Best
Friends Ever

A Dress for the Opera and True Friendship

I was twelve when I went shopping for my first fancy dress—something proper for the Salzburg Opera Festival. My mom and I bought the dress together. Mom picked it out and I adored it. It was buttercup yellow, with a tight bodice and a pleated skirt with a green velvet belt. I'll never forget how beautiful I felt prancing into the opera in the yellow dress I had bought with my mom.

Today, I still shop with my mom. But I pick out my clothes and she adores them (or doesn't). Today, since I'm older (forty-five, actually), my mom and I are more like friends. This friendship between mothers and children appears to be more natural and universal than magical and unique.

But still, because each of us lives only our own life, there is that seemingly magic and unique moment at eighteen or twenty-three or thirty-one when you suddenly realize that the woman who ran your life is now your peer. Suddenly, mom and kid are friends.

Friendship with our moms occurs in just the simple everyday things—going shopping, going to the movies, talking on the phone. The distance between friend and mother is just an instant, a moment of growth.

Isabel

Eisen and her daughter Leslie have an intense friendship built on love and trust. Mother and daughter finish each other's sentences and share the same big, beautiful smiles and warm, sparkly eyes. They are a joy to be around. Leslie, at age twenty-seven, is finding what her mom has known for a while—that her mom is her best friend.

My Mother, My Best Friend

My mother's a character. When I was growing up, she took me out of school every Tuesday because that was my mom and dad's day off. We would all get in the car and go have a picnic somewhere, usually a state park. We'd set the table with leaves if it were fall, flowers for spring.

She gave me an incredible appreciation for beauty, and she encouraged me to always have a pencil and paper around so I could draw. She taught me not only to draw nature but also to have a real appreciation of it, and my love of flowers comes from her. Even when I didn't have much money, I always bought myself flowers. My mother taught me to touch and to see and to listen. She taught me opera by playing the piano after dinner.

She heightened my senses; she taught me never to be bored by teaching me how to be by myself.

My mother had no money, but she saved and kept what she had in her pantyhose. When I first separated from my ex-husband and was in terrible shape, she said, "You know, you need to get away from everything. You need to be near the ocean." And she took me on a Princess cruise. We walked, talked, went on excursions, and met lovely people on the ship. We got dressed up, we bought trinkets, and she got me two massages. We were like best friends. I don't know if I felt like a new person after the trip, but I was certainly a rejuvenated one. That trip was the nicest thing she could have done for me, and she never once mentioned how expensive it was.

"She gave me an incredible appreciation for beauty."

My mother looks fabulous. She's very pretty and has fabulous skin. But she wears too much makeup, which she buys at Bendel, MAC, still, even though she's eighty-five!

She's a very unique lady.

—Isabel Eisen, EQUITY RESEARCH ANALYST

My Mom, My Best Friend

My mom is my best friend. She's unbelievable. I'm in love with her. She's wonderful and one of the most patient women I know—always able to deal with my stubbornness!

There's an incredible, unique bond between us. I think it developed during my toddler years, when I would *never* leave her side. We don't look alike, but our mannerisms—how we laugh, how we smile—are the same. We tell each other anything, even if we know it won't make the other one happy. We accept each other—we don't judge.

My mother and I like to travel together. When I was little, every Christmas she and I would travel to New York from Milwaukee, where we lived, and we would literally shop until we dropped. (My mother can outshop *anyone*.) We'd stay with my uncle, who lived at 80th and Park, and we'd walk all the way downtown and back again. It was so much fun. To this day, I associate New York with her, which is one of the reasons I moved here.

And when I was older, just a couple of years ago, we went to the Caribbean together. And, again, we had so much fun. We shared a room, and she would be back in the room at midnight and I'd come in at four in the morning and it was cool. She'd then make me get up at eight and we'd have breakfast together and I'd tell her about my night!

"She's fallen crazy in love and she gets all giddy."

My mother loves romance, and she's always preached to me the value of marriage. Yet she's also a strong woman who has always wanted me to work hard and be independent. I actually respect both her dependence *and* independence.

We're real accepting of each other. We respect each other, but in the past few years, as I've gotten older, the roles have reversed sometimes. She's fallen crazy in love and I now listen to her stories. And she gets all giddy and I'm the one saying, "Are you being careful?"

My mom is beautiful. She's reversed the aging process. She looks younger now than she did a few years ago.

And my mom's always smiling. And I'm always smiling.

—Leslie Eisen, SALESPERSON

Laughing in Church

I'm thirty-one. My mom is only eighteen years older than me, so she is more like a sister and a friend than a mom. I remember as a kid when my sister, Heather, my mom, and I would go to church. My sister and I would constantly get the giggles (for no reason other than we weren't supposed to laugh in church). Then my mom would start laughing too. With the three of us trying to hold in our laughs, the whole bench would shake.

My mom also taught us how to do cartwheels. Overall it was a lot of fun.

Michelle Friedman,
ART DIRECTOR

Cristina

Ferrare first became famous as a glamorous cover girl after a family friend told Cristina's mom, Renata, to introduce her fourteen-year-old to a well-known modeling agent. The model matured into an author and talk show host after surmounting the difficult end of her marriage to auto executive John DeLorean, father of the stillborn DeLorean sports car. Today, happily remarried for sixteen years to Tony Thomopoulos, she is busy with a wide variety of work, including a jewelry business she runs with her mom.

Love, Humor, Passion, and Food

We didn't have money growing up, and yet my mother made everything so much fun—and so perfectly normal and happy. She gave my siblings and me an upbringing filled with love, humor, passion, and food. I have such admiration and respect for my mother. She's my best friend in the whole world. She made raising three kids look effortless. She did it all. I don't know how she did it—*I* can't do it.

I have so many memories of my mother. Especially Sundays. We're Italian, and Sunday was a big day because the whole family would come over. I'd wake up every Sunday to the music of Mario Lanza and Tony Bennett on the record player and smell the sauce for dinner cooking in the kitchen. To this day, whenever I hear Tony Bennett my mouth starts to salivate because I think of the dinner that will follow! And that's where I think I got my love of cooking and family—from her.

There are so many ways my mother inspired me. She had—and still has—a very strong moral fiber. She's very spiritual, and her spirituality has grounded me, especially in tough times. When my ex-husband was arrested, I went through a very difficult six years. Without my mom and my family and my spiritual beliefs I don't think I could have lived through it. My mother and father and sister and brother were really incredible. And I don't think my siblings would have been so loving and supportive if my mother hadn't always demanded that we love and respect each other.

"My mother always demanded that we love and respect each other."

—Cristina Ferrare,

AUTHOR, TELEVISION PERSONALITY,

AND JEWELRY DESIGNER

James James Morrison's First Commandment

James James
Said to his Mother,
"Mother," he said, said he:
"You must never go down to the end of the town, if you don't go down with me."

—A. A. Milne,
AUTHOR OF WINNIE-THE-POOH

Source: A. A. Milne, *When We Were Very Young*
(New York: E.P. Dutton & Co., 1924).

Jan

Miller is a high-powered author's agent and a wonderful woman. As an agent, she has come to represent the authors of some of the best-selling self-help books. She has incredible warmth and a direct, no-nonsense approach to life—which she learned from her mom.

Bad Hair, Great Mom

My mother is a rock—so strong, so sure of who she is. She's been the best female role model. When I was thirteen years old she wrote me a letter that said: "Put your comb away. I thought you'd be a leader and you seem to be a follower. You need to take charge." My husband carries the letter around with him because he knows that someday he'll have to give his daughter the same advice.

She has a huge sense of humor. She's very energetic, has a terrific attitude about life, and is very achievement-oriented. She let me create my own style. She didn't give me the "you can't do this, you can't do that." In high school, she let me wear a blue jean jacket with my prom dress. It probably looked like hell, but she said, "You know, it looks pretty good to me. I kind of like the look."

My mother's always been perceptive, and she never put up with any bullshit. I'll never forget when I was in college and I received a "Dear Jan" letter. I was devastated—I leave for Christmas vacation and my boyfriend sends me a letter breaking up with me! My mom was very sympathetic. She could tell my heart was broken. I moped around and moped around, but after about three days, she came into my room and said, "All right, now, that's enough! You are now disrupting the whole family's Christmas. I'm sorry he did this to you, but this is what happens at this point in your life. Trust me, this guy will be back, and you won't be interested in him. Right now you are acting like a loser. He has the upper hand now and so much power—how could you give up your power?" Little did I know I'd one day be doing all these self-help books.

> "She has always been my friend first."

Then she said, "If you don't snap out of it, I'm packing your bags and you can go back to school ahead of schedule." And boom, I snapped out of it, and that was that. And she was right: He did come back, and I wasn't interested. And she taught me such a great lesson: that my behavior affects others, and it's not fair having one person disrupt an entire family.

I'm in awe of my mother. She's eighty now and still really active. She's fun, adorable, and funny, and she has always been my friend first. She says stuff to me like, "You act young, you look young, you wear great clothes, how come your hair looks like shit?" I love my mom.

—Jan Miller, AUTHOR'S AGENT

A Real Star

The only person I know who is stronger than I am—and more stubborn—is my mom. When I was growing up, she cleaned people's houses during the day and cleaned a motel at night. She also raised ten children.

And people try to tell me that playing two sports is hard.

—Bo Jackson,
ATHLETE

Source: Bo Jackson and Dick Schapp, *Bo Knows Bo* (New York: Doubleday, 1990).

Pretending

together can be a wonderful thing for mothers and kids. Dana Horn remembers it as a special way to keep her family close.

The Ip Family

I was able to see at an early age why my mom was so great. You see, she passed away when both she and I were young. It was only three years ago; I was twenty. We had reached a point where she was my best friend. I believe she was the one person who knew everything there is to know about me. I still believe she is my best friend, even though she isn't here.

My mom was like a kid—she never lost that quality. So I could always relate to her as a peer and as a mother. Sometimes we'd go out and I'd forget I was with my mom. As I grew up, the line between mother and daughter became blurred more and more.

Instead of telling me I was immature and to grow up, she encouraged my imagination. This might sound crazy, but for my entire life my mom and I pretended that my stuffed animals were real. She would make them talk to me and my brother, Josh. It was wonderful.

The stuffed animal thing really started when I was in fifth grade. My grandmother bought me a stuffed dog, and I named it Chip. It was a golden retriever, very ploppy. A few months later my brother got one. And then, while my mom was on vacation, she bought this really, really big one, that cost, like, a hundred dollars. We then had this stuffed animal dog family. It was something the three of us—my mom, my brother, and I—shared.

"My mom was like a kid—she never lost that quality."

They were the Ip family, because we named them all with names that ended in the letters "ip." Mom's was Pip and later she got Clip, and Josh had Flip and Zip. Even when I went to college, my mom would call me and put Pip on the phone. It was a real bond, something very special that I shared with my mom.

I still have the stuffed animals. I look at them and think of my mom and get a really warm, loving feeling. I miss my mom, but they make it easier.

—Dana Horn, ASSISTANT TELEVISION PRODUCER

Fred

Morrison and his wife, the former Helen Westergaard, named their only child Jeanette Helen. Janet Leigh, as the studio named her, went on to star in numerous films, including Psycho, *where she is best remembered being stabbed in the shower. She was married four times, most famously to actor Tony Curtis, and their daughter, Jamie Lee Curtis, born in 1958, became as famous as her parents.*

Mom and Me

I have many thoughts about my mom. Obviously I have great love for her. And a deep gratitude. She was the most selfless person I've ever known. Everything was for Daddy or me or someone else, never for her.

Grandma and Grandpa Westergaard emigrated from Denmark and raised their five children in northern California. There wasn't much money.

Fred Morrison and Helen Westergaard married young—too young—and Jeanette came along soon after. Neither had a proper education, and their mutual aim was to make sure their baby girl had the opportunity they had missed. They both worked hard from the beginning. Fortunately, Jeanette was an excellent student and also worked after school and in the summers to make the dream possible. Because Jeanette skipped grades, she graduated high school at fifteen and she was a college senior at eighteen.

A miracle happened in 1946 that changed the Morrisons' future. Jeanette became Janet Leigh, and the days of poverty were over—not all at once, but the road ahead was a lot smoother.

The sun shone brightly. Fred and Helen were proud and thrilled. They accompanied their daughter to celebrate the first Stockton "Janet Leigh Day." In a sense the honor was theirs more than hers. It was a happy time!

"She was the most selfless person I've ever known."

As Janet went on with her life, and Fred developed a small business, Helen suddenly was lost, with nothing to do. Sadly, in living for everyone else, she had neglected to find her own life, her own identity.

Mom, please know that your dedication and devotion are an inherent, integral reason for my existence, my beliefs, my person.

Thank you,

Jeanette

—Jeanette Helen Morrison, AKA JANET LEIGH

Friends

There is a point where you aren't as much mom and daughter as you are adults and friends. It doesn't happen for everyone—but it did for Mom and me.

—Jamie Lee Curtis, ACTRESS, MOTHER, AUTHOR

Source: *Mothers & Daughters*
(White Plains: Peter Pauper Press, 1998).

Helene

Rottenberg's mom wanted to be the best mom ever and, like many moms, she succeeded. She succeeded at being a great friend, too.

I Want to Be Sixty-five

All my mother wanted to do in life was to have kids. Her great goal was to be a great mom. What gives my mom pleasure is giving us stuff, buying us things, and doing stuff for us.

When I was getting divorced, she would call me every day and say, "Hello. I love you. Just checking to see how you're doing. Are the kids okay? Is everyone okay?" Ever since the divorce she and my dad have been coming over every Thursday to take care of my kids. Thursdays are really nice—I come home from work and the kitchen's clean and dinner's here! She's been doing that for seven years now. My mom is great.

We went out recently for my birthday and Mother's Day, which are around the same time, and I asked her, "If you could pick any age, what age would you choose?" (She's seventy-two, so I thought she'd want to be young.) Well, she picked sixty-five! And when I asked her why, she said, "Because I was really healthy then, and I had grandchildren." What a wonderful thing to say, that her grandchildren meant so much to her. It made me cry.

—Helene Rottenberg,
CLASSICAL GUITARIST, YOGA INSTRUCTOR,
AND PROFESSOR OF MUSIC

Our Moms Are the Best Role Models Ever

White Socks and Real Freedom

At a time when most women were taught to care more about cooking than college, my mom went to Radcliffe (when Harvard wouldn't admit women!) and never cooked or sewed. At a time when nylons were the rage and real women never wore socks, my mom insisted on white cotton socks because they were comfortable.

The socks embarrassed me terribly when I was eight and I was sure my friends would never speak to the daughter of a white-sock mom. But today, people tell me my wildly curly hair, idiosyncratic clothes, and multiple silver bracelets make a unique statement, and I know I've benefited greatly from my childhood embarrassment.

Our Moms Are the Best Role Models Ever

In a thousand ways, my mother and my generation's mothers modeled for their children an attitude of independence that they really didn't have. Somehow, my mom had the foresight to know there would be opportunities for me that had escaped most of her generation. So she prepared me to grab those opportunities whenever and wherever they appeared.

The amazing result of our mothers' attitudes and examples is that we did become more independent than our mothers. We were able to make career and personal choices that weren't available to our mothers. And the mothering miracle of our age is that our moms granted us independence without jealousy and gave us the future without remorse.

To all these moms, you have raised a generation of women and men who are able to follow their hearts and minds in their own way, along their own paths. You are the best role models ever.

Some

half a century ago, a carpenter and a burlap bag salesman in Toledo do business and brag about their kids. As a result, the kids get married and a new family forms. There's a divorce and life is disrupted, yet the mom is able to model for her children the simple truth of our connectedness to one another.

My Mother, the Doctor

My mother's a pediatrician. She was born in 1924, the youngest of six children. She had three sons—Steve, Len, and me, Richard, the middle son—and she raised us by herself in the 1960s.

Life with my mother was interesting and fascinating. She instilled in us a sense of social activism and commitment to the community. In 1964, we moved back to Toledo, where her family was from, and there she had us working on every political campaign in Cleveland and Toledo. We worked on the campaign of Carl Stokes, the first black mayor of Cleveland, at least two or three times. My mom would have us canvass the white and Italian neighborhoods on the east side of Cleveland, supporting and promoting Carl. We'd troll through the neighborhoods, and I'd deliver various position papers and things like that. Sometimes we'd talk to people door to door.

We all went to the Cleveland Symphony together. We would get dressed up and be Mom's date. The week before we went, she would have us take the records out from the library, listen to the pieces, and read about the composers. After the symphony we would go to Howard Johnson's for peppermint stick ice cream.

"Anything that's good about me I probably got from my mother."

We got the Sunday *Times* and the daily *Cleveland Plain Dealer* delivered, and at dinner every evening it was expected that we'd have read and be able to discuss the editorials. On Sundays we were expected also to have read the *Week in Review*. Starting in elementary school she would ask us questions like, "Do you think Morris Udall is the best Democratic candidate?" (It was a given that we were left-wing liberal Democrats.) She wasn't grilling us. There was just an expectation that part of becoming an adult was being informed. I'm very grateful to her for that.

My mother gave me the sense that humankind is tribal, that you look out for each other, that we're all connected, and that we're trying to get it right. And that we're never going to get it totally right but that we should keep trying and thinking about it—learning about history, learning from history, and not making the mistakes from history. At forty-three, I can get pretty jaded, but I don't think she ever did.

Today, my brothers are both doctors. Steve's a radiologist in Houston and Len's a family practitioner in rural Maryland. I'm a professor. And anything that's good about me I probably got from my mother.

"My mother gave me the sense that humankind is tribal, that you look out for each other, that we're all connected."

—Richard Sax, DEAN OF ARTS AND HUMANITIES,
Madonna University, Livonia, Michigan

Believing in Magic

My mother always seemed to me a fairy princess, a radiant being possessed of limitless riches and power.

—Sir Winston Churchill,
PRIME MINISTER OF GREAT BRITAIN
1940–1945 and 1951–1955

Source: Lucy Mead, *Mothers Are Special* (New York: Gramercy Books, 2000).

Evans's mom was her biggest role model. Gail's book, Play Like a Man, Win Like a Woman, *begins with this tribute to her mom: "When it comes to role models, I was lucky." Now Gail's daughter, Julianna, looks to her for the same courageous support. Gail and Julianna are also the closest of friends.*

A Recipe for Role Modeling

My mother was strong and very decisive. She knew what she liked and what she didn't. She taught me that women can have fulfilling, interesting lives; that I could do anything. Which is really funny because she also sent the message that you have to marry a good man, be a good wife and mother, and do the conventional things. She came from that era, when a woman supported her husband no matter what. Basically, my mother thought that you could be anything you wanted to be as long as you kept your husband happy.

One of the things that she did, and the one that she was proudest of, was teaching at the Guild for the Blind in New York. She started a class teaching blind people how to sew and make crafts so they could earn money. And every year she would have a fashion show, where her students would model the clothes they had made. For my mother, teaching people how to be self-sufficient was much more enjoyable than serving on a fund-raising committee.

My mother was really committed to this idea of helping people have better lives. She also worked for the Hawthorne School for juvenile delinquents, and every other weekend she would bring home one of her students to spend time with us. I recently heard from one of them. He's seventy now, but when he was fourteen years old, he was a twelve-time loser. He really turned his life around: He became a military security person and he once served as head of telecommunications security for the Reagan-Gorbachev summit in Reykjavik.

"I never had to go searching for someone else's mom or sister to have a role model as a woman; my mom was the best role model ever."

Dedicated as she was to catering to her husband, when my best interests were at stake, my mother would make exceptions. One of the few times she actually spoke back to my dad in front of me was when I was choosing a college. My father very much wanted me to go someplace conventional, like Smith. But my mother and I had met the admission officers from Bennington, a much more liberal school at the time, and we had agreed to go see it on our college tour.

When we got back from visiting Bennington, my mom said to my dad, "We found this wonderful place; it's where Gail is going to go to college." And my father said, "No way. She's not going to a place like that." And my mother looked my father right in the eye and said, "If we haven't taught her the difference between right and wrong by now, we'll never be able to teach her. She's going to Bennington."

For me it was a very pivotal moment: I would have been a very different person had I not gone to Bennington, which really encouraged me to think differently from the conservative schooling I had had up until then.

I never had to go searching for someone else's mom or sister to have a role model as a woman; my mom was the best role model ever. I often made her nervous when I pushed the envelope, which I did a lot. But I know she also loved it. Seeing my mom take joy in my struggles to grow, having my mom's faith and courage as a standard, has allowed me to allow my daughter to become the woman she wants to be.

—Gail Evans, CNN EXECUTIVE VICE PRESIDENT AND AUTHOR

Psychic Ability to Guide Me

I feel inspired by my mother's success. Since I was a little kid, I've known that she's really sharp and amazing and could handle a lot of stuff, but it has never intimidated me. It's actually comforting: Because of her I know *I* can do it; I can be successful, too. I'm learning from her by osmosis—just by being around her and being part of her life. I've always liked being around people who make an impact, and I love the fact that my mother is the biggest wheeler and dealer of them all.

She's very easy to talk to, and she's always available for me. From "What should I do about this guy?" to "What job should I take?" she has an incredible, almost psychic ability to guide me to the right decisions. I value her judgment more than anyone else's in my life.

Three years ago, when I was twenty-six, I took a year off to travel and write a book. I was very hesitant to do it at first, but when I asked her what she thought, she didn't blink twice, saying, "Do it! You have the rest of your life for your career. Go after your heart and your passion." It was the same thing with my present job. I was working for *Time* magazine in a very established, good career job, and I had the chance to go to an Internet company. I was really unsure about making the leap, but my mother just felt it made sense, that there would be lots of opportunity, and she was 100 percent correct. It's been the perfect job for me.

"I really enjoy her company. She's fun and goofy."

I really enjoy her company. She's fun and goofy. (Actually I'm more the goofy one, but she's still goofy.) I like teasing her and playing with her. She's very smart—not only news savvy and book smart, but she's got a sharp eye and a really keen sense of who people are and how they work. I like spending time with her. She's easy company. When I'm with my mother, a day without a plan is still a good plan. She'll say to me, "Hey, I've got some dry cleaning to pick up. Will you come with me?" And I go with her, because she can make the mundane appealing. I don't even know what we talk about in the car; I just love spending time with her. She's such a valuable part of my life.

—Juliana Evans, PUBLIC RELATIONS MANAGER FOR ETOUR.COM

No Complaints

I don't recall [her] ever griping a lot. She's a strong lady. She wasn't a griper . . .

—Clint Eastwood,

ACTOR, DIRECTOR

Source: Lucy Mead, *Mothers Are Special* (New York: Gramercy Books, 2000).

Having

talent is not always enough. Sometimes we need someone to teach us what to do with it. Robin Liles's mom gave her the gift of creativity—teaching her how to open her eyes and turn ordinary things into extraordinary ornaments.

Rescuing Tumbleweeds

When I think of my mother, I see her as a creative Renaissance woman. She paints beautiful Southwestern landscapes, can sew anything you can imagine, decorates with flair, and boy, can she throw a party with style.

Based on this long-standing reputation, she was put in charge of setting up my kindergarten class's Christmas tree. I grew up on the Gulf Coast, in Lake Jackson, Texas, which is about an hour south of Houston. Contrary to what most people think, Texas has lots of differing landscapes. This part of Texas is very wooded, green, and extremely humid. It was the 1970s and my class at Oran M. Roberts Elementary School was ill-prepared for the jaw-dropping alternative to the typical fake fir she would provide us with.

On our way back through West Texas after a trip to my grandparents' in New Mexico a couple of weeks prior to the holiday, she mystified my family when she pulled off the side of the road to "rescue" a tumbleweed that had rolled into our path. Hauling it back to my classroom, she spray-painted it gold and hung lots of red Christmas balls on it. It was so simple, gorgeous, and purely "Texas"—and such a hit with our group of five-year-olds, most of whom had never seen a tumbleweed before. Everyone told me what a genius my mom was, and she still has that effect on people. Martha Stewart, eat your heart out!

"Martha Stewart, eat your heart out!"

—Robin Liles, GRAPHIC DESIGNER

Do Right

My mother, Josephine Brown Johnson, has been the most important influence on my life. Her consistent message to me was "Work hard. Do right. And you will succeed."

She earned a high school diploma, was married to my father at age sixteen, and worked most of her life six days a week in a small neighborhood grocery store owned by my uncle. My dad was in poor health most of my life, leaving Mother as the primary provider.

Her example taught me the value of hard work and a good education. My early life experiences also ignited a burning desire in me to excel.

Today Mother is ninety-three and still living in our hometown in Macon, Georgia.

—Tom Johnson,
CHAIRMAN AND CHIEF EXECUTIVE OFFICER, CNN

The

title "Mahatma" means "great-souled," and Mohandas Gandhi always hated it, thinking it much too grand and pretentious for a simple man like himself. The man who perfected peaceful, nonviolent civil disobedience and used it to free a subcontinent, Gandhi's greatest virtue often seemed his ability to patiently wait for the sun of freedom to shine on his people in its own good time. As it turns out, waiting for the sun to shine was a virtue learned from his mother.

A Saint's Saint

The outstanding impression my mother has left on my memory is that of saintliness. She was deeply religious. She would not think of taking her meals without her daily prayers . . . As far as my memory can go back, I do not remember her having ever missed the Chaturmas [the four-month-long Hindu season of fasting during the rainy season in India].

She would take the hardest vows and keep them without flinching. Illness was no excuse for relaxing them. I can recall her once falling ill when she was observing [a fast], but the illness was not allowed to interrupt the observance. To keep two or three consecutive fasts was nothing to her. Living on one meal a day during Chaturmas was a habit with her. Not content with that, she fasted every alternate day during one Chaturmas.

During another Chaturmas she vowed not to have food without seeing the sun. We children on those days would stand, staring at the sky, waiting to announce the appearance of the sun to our mother. Everyone knows that at the height of the rainy season the sun often does not condescend to show his face. And I remember days when, at his sudden appearance, we would rush and announce it to her. She would run out to see with her own eyes, but by that time the fugitive sun would be gone, thus depriving her of her meal.

"That does not matter," she would say cheerfully. "God did not want me to eat today." And then she would return to her round of duties.

—Mahatma Gandhi, INDIAN POLITICAL LEADER, 1869–1948

Source: Mohandas Gandhi,
Gandhi's Autobiography:
The Story of My Experiments with Truth
(Washington: Public Affairs Press, 1948).

The Model of Grace

My mother, moving gracefully through the house and garden, arranging flowers, breakfasting on a white wicker tray in her bedroom, was easily the most beautiful creature imaginable. Her voice was soft, with a light Irish accent. She seemed possessed of magical qualities and an unending supply of stories. At night I lay in bed listening for the rustle of silk or taffeta, waiting for her perfume to overpower the scent of jasmine.

—Mia Farrow, ACTRESS

Source: Alice Faye Cleese and Brian Bates,
How to Manage Your Mother
(New York: Regan Books, 1999).

Our Moms Are the Most Fun Ever

Mom, Mayhem, and Real People

Mothers—apart from being mothers—are people, too. We know they were people before they became mothers, but we sometimes forget. On rare occasions, we even got glimpses of our moms being people while we were still young, usually when we were up past our curfews!

Our mothers, like other real people, can be quirky sometimes. They can get elated for reasons that their children do not understand, and they can be struck by weird moods and fits, just like the kids.

Very often, the quirkiness of our moms comes out in moments of great fun and extraordinary zaniness—my mom and I raced lobsters down the kitchen hall! Moms can be sources of great fun, and great joy, even as they put up with our funny moods, our spilled spaghetti, and our bratty temperaments.

The following stories are moms at their funniest and most unpredictable selves. This section is for the whimsical and wacky, most fun moms ever.

Christina

Clarke's mom participated in water fights in the kitchen and loved the story that follows. She told it at nearly every gathering she went to for the last twenty years of her life.

Monkey Business

From cats and geese to disenfranchised teenagers, my mother was always taking in strays, and as a result, our house was a confusing, noisy, hilarious place to grow up. But the uninvited monkey pushed the boundaries of even my mother's liberal open-door policy.

When I was ten years old, I awoke one morning just in time to make the school bus. Rubbing my very nearsighted eyes, I walked into the bathroom to hear a strange, insistent scratching sound, which became increasingly louder and more insistent the longer I stayed. Although visually impaired, I finally located its source: Two feet above my head, a monkey sat atop the wall-mounted lighting fixture. I promptly ran from the room screaming at the top of my lungs, "Mom, there's a monkey in the bathroom."

She, of course, didn't believe me. Why would she? We lived in suburban Long Island.

She shooed me off to school and placated my sobs by admitting the possibility that perhaps a squirrel had gotten into the house during the night, although she didn't really believe that, either. Two of my siblings came down separately to grab their lunch bags for school and, one after the other, casually mentioned to my mother as they ran out the door that there was a monkey swinging down the banister. My mom went upstairs and told my father, who was brushing his teeth, that the kids had said there was a monkey swinging around the house. Without taking the brush from his mouth, he said, "Doesn't surprise me; this house is a zoo!"

"Our house was a confusing, noisy, hilarious place to grow up."

After my dad left the house for work (without even bothering to check the lamp fixtures or banisters), my mom went into her room to make her bed and was shocked by the sight of a two-foot-high, brown-haired monkey swinging from rung to rung on her bed canopy.

Half an hour later my mother was at the local Garden Club regaling very proper ladies with her tales of how she had tried to lure the monkey with a banana, only to have it spit back at her with simian ungratefulness. Stunned, they asked her why she left a monkey alone in the house. Confused, she said because she had to leave to come to the meeting. Unnerved, they made her leave to go save her home from wild monkeys. She came home to find torn curtains, broken lamps, and banana peels everywhere.

The skeptical policeman covered the phone during her call and yelled to the squad room, "We got a lady here says there's a monkey in the house." And when he got back on the phone, he advised, "Lady, when you catch that monkey, call a pet store!"

P.S. The pet store owner finally came and took the captured monkey (lured back into the bathroom with more bananas). And the neighbor's response to Mom's rendition was, "I saw that monkey in the neighborhood a week ago; I knew he'd end up at the Lamberts'!"

—Christina Lambert Clarke, EDITOR AND WRITER
(with forgotten details and editing supplied
by big sister Peggy Lambert)

A Richness of Spirit

A rich child often sits in the lap of a poor mother.

—Spanish proverb

E.C.

Mahon's mom keeps things in perspective by following her impulses—and makes life fun for her children in the process.

Mom Rules!

ere are just a handful of the reasons why my mom rules:

- She believes in satisfying cravings.
  Sometimes when I call her at work she's eating french fries and a chocolate milkshake at her desk for lunch—and she always let us have chocolate cake for breakfast if we had any in the house. She's a skinny little thing but she doesn't have any food issues. Gotta love that!

- She doesn't take things overly seriously.
  When I was a teenager and the dirtiest and most rebellious music I owned was the Violent Femmes, my mom let us play it in the car—and sang along!

- She's not jaded.

  Even though we live in New York City, she uses the expression "What the Sam Hill?" and says "Dead, Tennessee Jed!" when she kills a bug. She talks to strangers and always rushes over to hold doors open for anyone with a baby stroller.

- She's a romantic.

  The American President was her favorite movie for a while. She saw it in the theater, then she would watch it on pay-per-view, and when it was the in-flight movie on three trips in a row, she rented the headphones all three times.

- She has an amazingly broad sense of humor.

  From corny jokes and puns to Woody Allen's and Dennis Miller's wry insights, she thinks everything is funny. But most of all, she thinks we're hilarious. My friends all adore her because she'll always sit with us for a while when they come over and roar at everything we say.

- She's the consummate shopper.

  Although she works like crazy, she spends like crazy—mostly on her friends and family. She believes that a two hundred–dollar haircut is an investment, that every occasion calls for gifts and party favors, and that running around looking for bargains is a waste of time (time being money, it cancels out whatever you would've saved). Her sisters accuse her of paying "retail plus 10 percent" for everything.

- She has great instincts.
  Besides her rock-solid common sense and business savvy, she has an incredible instinct for seeing through people. She can smell a rat a mile away and her gut reactions always turn out to be right on target. She's the best advisor on everything from etiquette to careers to love, but she tends to keep her love advice fairly spare; she hates to meddle.

- She thinks her kids are great.
  And the feeling is mutual!

—E. C. Mahon, BOOK EDITOR AND NEW MOM

Sweet Winter Memories

When I was a child and the snow fell, my mother always rushed to the kitchen and made snow ice cream and divinity fudge—egg whites, sugar, and pecans, mostly. It was a lark then and I always associate divinity fudge with snowstorms.

—Eudora Welty

Source: *New Yorker*, February 18, 1985.

Sometimes,

through humor, our moms reveal the truth about our character. And sometimes, they're just making mischief!

No One Stole the Gum?

When I was only four years old my mother called me, my older brother, and my older sister into the kitchen and asked which one of us took the packs of gum from the cupboard. We all looked at each other innocently, shrugged our shoulders, and said, "It wasn't me, Mom."

Throughout our lives my mom would bring up the gum story, and we would joke and tease one another about the incident. Nobody ever confessed, and each one of us always wondered who really did take it, and why they didn't just confess already! (Hey, I was only four at the time, I maintained, and didn't even know there was any gum in the cupboard.)

Many years later, at the (too young) age of fifty-four, my mother, my best friend, passed away from lung cancer. To the end, she kept her sense of humor, spunk, and wit. Two weeks before she died, she called me to her side and said, "Christine, I need to tell you something. There wasn't ever any gum. I just wanted to see how you all would handle yourselves." She said she wanted to know if we would blame one another and if we would stick to our stories.

"It wasn't me, Mom."

"Oh, and by the way," she continued (since she was in a confessing mood), "I didn't make that delicious sausage bread for your father's Christmas parties. He bought it from an Italian deli!"

Mom, I love you dearly.

—Christine McGovern,
MOTHER OF MATTHEW, CONNOR, AND JACK

Eat, Drink, and Make Merry

Of course I don't always enjoy being a mother. At those times my husband and I hole up somewhere in the wine country, eat, drink, make mad love, and pretend we were born sterile and raise poodles.

—Dorothy DeBolt,

NATURAL MOTHER OF SIX AND
ADOPTIVE MOTHER OF FOURTEEN

Source: *San Francisco Chronicle*, April 22, 1980.

Anywhere

you go in the world, moms are amazingly similar. Whether from Toledo, Chicago, or China, our moms' ability to make life fun is what our memories are made of. Mary Mo Yen Wu's Mama Wu has a capacity for mystery, fun, and life itself that has baffled even scientists!

Mamu Wu

Some say a loving mother would die for her children. My mother did just the opposite! She lived for them. Just after giving birth to me, her third child, Mama Wu went into a Code Blue coma. While being revived, she made the decision to live so she could raise her children. Since that time she has endured an almost endless series of medical conditions, and how she pulls through each time is a medical mystery! One of her doctors once described her as a "walking Murphy's Law."

My mother left China and came to the U.S. when she was my age, twenty-six. She went to school, worked, married the one and only love of her life, and raised a deaf daughter to speak with her own voice. She fought discrimination. She traveled all over the world, became computer literate, and volunteered in countless capacities in her community. She has lived an unselfish life because of her faith.

I remember moments of pure lightheartedness and joy with my mother, moments like taking us fishing for blue gills, baiting our hooks. Camping all over the country, cooking ramen noodles on the fire, all the while singing in Chinese, broken English, and sign language. Sewing matching plaid and bold print outfits for all of us. Filming all these moments on Super 8mm, then Betamax, then VHS tapes.

"More than just loving her, I genuinely like her."

She was always taking shortcuts that took twice as long. I remember her driving me to piano and Chinese lessons in the station wagon with wood side panels; giving us Flintstones vitamins; spanking us when we deserved it; hugging us a lot; and always supporting or encouraging what made us happy.

Once she made dinosaur eggs for us by emptying out little gelatin capsules and putting tiny pictures of dinosaurs inside them. She used to cut Twinkies in thirds for us to share. She played mah-jongg and video games with us, bought us the deluxe fast-food Play Doh set, and snuck homemade popcorn into the movie theater when we went to see *Return of the Jedi.*

Without dispute I believe Mama Wu should top the Best Mom Ever list, and more than just loving her, I genuinely like her.

—Mary Mo Yen Wu, INDUSTRIAL DESIGNER

Recreational Cooking

My mother was a good recreational cook, but what she basically believed about cooking was that if you worked hard and prospered, someone else would do it for you.

—Nora Ephron

Source: James B. Simpson, *Simpson's Contemporary Quotations* (Boston: Houghton Miffllin Company, 1988).

Holiday

traditions often spark magical memories of fun, love, and family. Lee Wilkins's mom still goes all out to make their family holidays delicious fun.

Pumpkins on TV

What really makes a mom a mom to me is how special she makes you feel every time you're around her. My mom has always made my brother and me feel like we're the center of her world. One way she does this is by making each holiday an event that someday, when I'm a dad, I will pass on to my children and always hold close to my heart for the rest my life.

I remember as a kid going to pick out a pumpkin for Halloween and how excited I'd get. We'd load up and head out to the best pumpkin patch or stand we could find, and then spend what seemed like an hour selecting the perfect pumpkin. Mine had to be bigger than my brother's. Once back home, the night's festivities would include watching scary movies, carving our pumpkins, baking the seeds (they taste *awesome*), and helping Mom make homemade chocolate oatmeal cookies—my favorite.

What really made the night, though, was the excitement and enthusiasm my mom would put into everything. She really made it fun! The last thing, and without a doubt the hit of the night, came when my mom would turn off all the lights, place our pumpkins on top of the TV, and light the candles inside them. It was so cool! In case you haven't guessed by now, Halloween is my favorite holiday. This truly was one of the best nights of the year.

"What really makes a mom a mom . . . is how special she makes you feel every time you're around her."

My mom seems to be an expert at making each holiday an unforgettable experience. I may be older now—all of thirty-three—but I go through the same traditions. Year after year, even to this day, I still look forward to the holidays with the same wide-eyed wonder I had as a kid. For this reason I consider my mom to be the best mom anyone could ever hope to have. Memories like this are what life is all about.

Oh yeah—and if you think Halloween was great, you should have seen my house around Christmas. *Wow!*

—Lee Wilkins, HUMAN RESOURCES DIRECTOR

Our
Moms
Are the Best
Teachers Ever

Tying Shoes and Being Yourself

Our mothers are our greatest teachers. They tend to teach us the really important stuff—the lessons that, once learned, allow us to become independent people with richer, more rewarding lives.

Moms teach us how to make a meal and a bed; how to pay a bill and a compliment; how to conduct a conversation and a relationship; how to say "thank you" and "I'm sorry."

My mother taught me how to tie my shoelaces and how to read and how to pay my bills. My mom also has taught me the not so obvious stuff—things like how to be respectful to others, how to be honest, and how to accept myself for who I am.

Moms Are the Best Teachers Ever

The voices that follow talk about moms who have taught them how to be strong, to stand up for themselves, to follow their dreams, to take care of others—all sorts of critical lessons. It is a tribute to the best teachers ever—our moms.

Judy

Collins has always had a strong sense of family and commitment to those close to her. It was her father's strong singing voice that first set Judy on a track to become one of her generation's shining stars, recording hits like "Both Sides Now" and "Amazing Grace." But her mother was also a strong and moving influence.

White Bubbles

The daily rituals of life can be the most enduring and touching—like washing, sewing, or singing.

I remember my mother as young and slim. She often wore graceful patent leather heels, white silk blouses tied in a bow at her throat, and ankle-length tweed skirts, the scent of Chanel No. 5 in her hair. She was a good-looking woman with big hazel eyes in which I always told her there were chunks of color that looked like fruitcake.

I can still feel my mother's strong fingers on my scalp, lathering shampoo into mounds of white bubbles in my hair. I would lie on my back on the steel kitchen counter, my head in the sink, as she rinsed my long blond hair with water and then vinegar to make it squeak and shine. When it was dry, she braided it and tied ribbons to the ends.

Mother made all my clothes for as long as I can remember. We poured over McCall's pattern book and shopped together for fabric. Neither of us spoke as she took in the seams and measured hems with her mouth full of pins, but in those quiet moments I often felt a closeness and love for my mother that made me weak in the knees.

"I often felt a closeness and love for my mother that made me weak in the knees."

My mother would play the piano and read me stories. When I was very young, I would stand in my Dr. Dentons and sing for my parents and their friends. "Charles," Mommy said to my father after I had sung my song, "it's way past Judy's bedtime." Left alone with him, I could convince my father to let me stay up later, but my mother could not be swayed and would make sure I got to bed on time. Still, I knew she loved to hear me sing.

I have a lifetime of memories. What stands out is that my mother did the best she could do. She taught me how to survive.

—Judy Collins, SINGER

Dr. Girl

When I was five years old, my best friend's mother asked what I wanted to be when I grew up. "I want to be a doctor," I said. "You can't be a doctor because you're a girl; you have to be a nurse," she said. "My mommy said I can be whatever I want to be," I told her. Now, twenty-six years later, I'm finally going to be Dr. Thomas, making house calls.

—Debi Thomas,

WORLD CHAMPION AND OLYMPIC FIGURE SKATER AND DOCTOR

Source: Kim Doren and Charlie Jones, *You Go Girl!* (Kansas City: Andrews McMeel, 2000).

Born

into an army family in Tulsa, Oklahoma, Judy Woodruff had lived in five states and two foreign countries by the time she was thirteen. During those years, it was her mother who held the family together and consistently advised her eldest daughter, Judy, to get an education and pursue her career.

Diapers and Dishes Can Wait

There are so many wonderful things about my mother.

She came from a family of very little means in Springfield, Missouri, and they moved to Tulsa, Oklahoma, when she was a little girl. She was the second of six children and her father, my grandfather, died when she was fourteen years old. So she quit school a year or so after that to stay home and help raise her younger siblings so her mother could work. She was incredibly selfless and generous with the love and care she gave to her family and particularly to her younger siblings.

She went to work, met my father, and was married when she was twenty-three years old. She was an elevator operator at one of the big oil company buildings downtown. She continued to work for a short period of time after I was born.

I have a memory from when I was three or four years old. It's one of my only real vivid memories of being little. We were living in Tulsa and my father, who was in the army, was pulling me in a wagon down the street to meet my mom as she was coming home from work.

She stopped working soon after that so she could care for me and my younger sister. She devoted all of her energy and time to us and to my father and the home. We moved around a lot, and my mother was the one who did everything. She held us together, literally, because I didn't like all these moves and I don't think she did either, but she put up with it. She kept the house going, prepared all the meals, furnished everything, even did a little sewing and gardening. She loved gardening.

"The thing that stands out to me is her incredible generosity."

The thing that stands out to me is her incredible generosity to me and my sister. There was a time when my family didn't have a great deal of money. I mean, my father was living on an army salary. She always made sure that my sister and I had money for school clothes and for whatever it was that we wanted. I know I didn't appreciate it at the time, but as an adult I've appreciated it just enormously. It makes me emotional to think about what she did for me and for my sister.

My mom was determined that I was going to get a college education, that I was going to have a career. She didn't want me rushing into any relationships, certainly not getting married and having kids too young. In high school, she was always telling me, "Diapers and dishes can wait. I want you to get an education." I had a lot of friends who had no intention of going to college, and if they were going, it was to meet someone and get married. But my mother hadn't gone to college—she hadn't even finished high school—and she was determined that I was going to get a college education and have a career. She kept saying over and over again, "Diapers and dishes can wait." I mean, it was this constant refrain. I remember that vividly. It makes me smile.

Obviously, my mother's advice affected me, because I graduated from Duke and didn't get married until I was thirty-three. And now I have this great career. She is very proud of that and I am very proud of her.

—Judy Woodruff, CNN NEWS ANCHOR

Wonderful Lessons

My mother shared with me many wonderful secrets:

To be in *the world but not* of *it.*

To look through the eyes of a child every day and recapture joy and beauty in simple things.

That love can truly be enough.

And that the greatest luxury in life is becoming a grandmother.

Thank you, Mom!

—June Nigro,
MOTHER, GRANDMOTHER, AND NANNY

The

legendary children's entertainer Shari Lewis was first discovered on the Arthur Godfrey Talent Scouts *show in 1952, working with an outsized wooden dummy who virtually dwarfed her own five-foot frame. Five years later, on the* Captain Kangaroo Show, *Lewis tried something more her own size and Lamb Chop, the diminutive sock puppet with a larger-than-life attitude, was born. In their later years, Shari and Lamb Chop were joined by Shari's daughter, Mallory, who helped write and produce the shows and specials that remained so vital, fresh, and popular even after some forty years. Shari died in 1998, but Lamb Chop lives on, thanks to Mallory's dedication to continuing her mother's work.*

A Letter to Mom

Dear Mommy,

Your grandson, Jamie, and I spent the evening reading. Thanks to you.

I remember when you read to me as I cuddled in your lap. Now I do that with my son. I remember when you took me on trips with you and Lamb Chop, making me feel special, folding origami toys for me, always making sure that I knew that I was the most important person in your world. Now I do that with my son.

Aunt Judy told me that she remembered how you were always teaching me as we played, pointing out pictures in my books, saying the names of the objects, and having me try to repeat them. Now I do that with my son.

I hold him, I sing to him, I tell him how smart he is, how funny, how loving, and how handsome. I do with Jamie all that you did with me. I just wish you could be here to see it.

It's only been in these last fifteen months as a mother that I finally come to understand that you *did* base your life around me, as much as you could, as often as possible. I recognize how hard you worked to balance your professional life, the rigors of show biz, with the demands of motherhood. I'm not a play-ground/carpool type mommy, either. But, like you, I crayon with my little guy. And, as I did, Jamie learns the names of his various body parts, and how to sing along and play along with joy. You didn't get to know him, but he and I are both lucky, as he already knows you. Grandma lives in the TV, I tell him, and in our hearts.

"You were the best mom ever, irreplaceable."

I have no regrets about our relationship; we were best friends and working companions. (Where am I gonna get such a great star to produce for again?) We had fun at the mall, on the phone, and on airplanes. But, Mom, you left too soon.

I was only eight weeks pregnant. I wish you could have stuck around to meet my baby. I wanted to put him in your arms, have you hold him, and tell me what a good job I did making him. I wanted you to know him, and to know me as a mother. I'm trying to be a great one, just like you.

I'm taking care of Lambie for you too, Mom, and for Jamie. You made sure she was a wonderful "little sister" to me, and I'll make sure she'll be a terrific "aunt" to him.

Mom, I really miss you. I miss holding your little hands, going to the ladies' room together, and borrowing your clothes. You are still so present in my life: I see outfits in stores that I reach for to buy you; I grab the phone to call you; and I order your favorite foods at dinner. I keep you close by, (finally) trying to be a grown-up: a good wife, a hard worker, and a loving mom. Thank you for showing me how, but I gotta tell you, your size fives leave big footsteps to follow.

You were the best mom ever, irreplaceable.

Until we meet again,

Your loving daughter,

Mally

—Mallory Lewis, TELEVISION PRODUCER

An Apple for My Mom

When Jimmy Carter was president, he called and said, "Loretta, we want you to come up here. Five famous people will come in and bring the teacher that has taught 'em the most." . . . So I told President Carter I couldn't bring a teacher. And he said, "Why?" I said, "Well, my mommy was what taught me most." And he said, "Well, there's always got to be a first. Bring her." That was the biggest thrill that my mother ever had.

—Loretta Lynn,
COUNTRY-WESTERN SINGER

Source: Suzanne Beilenson, *Mothers & Daughters* (White Plains: Peter Pauper Press, 1988).

Laurence

Margolis is an attorney who learned from his mother the importance of being involved in his community and helping others. These lessons his mother taught him have shaped his life.

Condoms, Drugs, and Alcohol

Nancy Kay Nupuf Margolis is my mom. To her, motherhood was not just a blessing but also a profound responsibility—another way for her to positively influence society. She would raise her children to take after her. So she emphasized a good work ethic and a compassionate and honest heart; she instilled in me the skills of independence necessary for adulthood, the need to seek higher education, to challenge convention, and to work to fulfill the greater good.

There were four kids in our family. I was the youngest. We were all assigned chores. At four years old, my mother showed me how doing the laundry could actually be fun and how I should learn to cook, especially because, as she would say, "Your father never did."

I grew up in the 1970s in Ann Arbor, Michigan. When I was eleven years old, to share with us her opening of an inner-city health clinic, she gave me a condom and explained to me the importance of it. She openly dealt with drugs and alcohol, knowing we would be better off if we experimented a little than we would if she just lectured abstinence. I really feel fortunate my parents were liberals. Their openness has made all the difference in my life.

> "Can we all have the greatest mother ever? Can this be possible? Are they all great? Well, sure."

Diversity and the importance of social causes were values my mother emphasized and continues to promote. At her behest I worked summers for a family shelter and volunteered at the hospital, on political campaigns, or with younger kids at the Jewish Community Center.

Due to the importance she (and my dad) placed on social causes, I became an attorney. I try to help people who face high hurdles and often cannot help themselves.

That's what it was like growing up for me and I thank God I had my mother.

Can we all have the greatest mother ever? Can this be possible? Are they all great? Well, sure. Because to each of us, our mothers represent the model from which others are judged—the perfect mother.

"To her, motherhood was not just a blessing but also a profound responsibility."

Nevertheless, objectively speaking (right?), I still think my mom is the greatest of 'em all.

—Laurence Margolis, ATTORNEY

A Strong Interest in the World

The greatest difference which I find between my mother and the rest of the people whom I have known is this, and it is a remarkable one: While others felt a strong interest in a few things, she felt a strong interest in the whole world and everything and everybody in it.

My mother had a great deal of trouble with me, but I think she enjoyed it.

—Mark Twain,
AUTHOR AND HUMORIST

Source: Alexandra Stoddard, *Mothers: A Celebration* (New York: William Morrow and Co. 1996).

Sharing

with her children the moral values of Judaism was important to Renee Burk's mother. Her devotion to her religious and social values caused Renee and her sisters to grow up strong and with their mom's beautiful spirit.

What's Really Important

My father came from Hungary as a very young man. When he felt it was time for him to marry, he went back to Hungary, met and married my mom, and brought her to this country. She was only twenty. I was born a year later. We lived in a little town in Texas—quite a difference from Budapest, the large, sophisticated city where she had grown up. But she made the adjustment.

My mom was a very strong, special woman. I got my sense of who I am, my love of books and music, and my religion from my mother. She was short and very pretty. And she always dressed; even doing housework she'd be all "put together." She had jewelry—nothing fancy, costume jewelry—but she wore it in a way that made it look special. She had a flair.

I have two sisters and we are very close today because of my mother. She taught us the importance of family, how to talk to each other and how to act. We find that we are always talking about our mother, remembering the things she taught us, the advice she gave us, the things she said and did, what she liked, her lovely manner. She was a very wise, dignified, and elegant lady—but also a woman with a sense of humor and a capacity for fun.

> "We remember the things she taught us, what she liked, her lovely manner."

She provided for us a great sense of our Jewish heritage, which she worked very hard to do. It was especially challenging and difficult because there were only six other Jewish families in our town. After working all day in Father's store, she would come home, prepare a beautiful Sabbath meal, and, after dinner, she became our teacher of Jewish history, philosophy, values, and prayers.

I remember our family Passover Seders. They were small Seders, but she still worked so hard at them, making the table very beautiful with a family heirloom embroidered white cloth. I remember the Hagudah that she marked to show the portion we would each read. It was so important to her that we understood our Jewish history.

Moral issues were very important to her, too, believing that these were the basic tenants of Judaism. And I remember one particular incident that was a very difficult lesson for me.

In school we had something called "declamations." It was a writing contest. All the kids would write something original and then stand up and read it. You were judged on the content of your writing and how well you spoke and presented it. And I won every year but one. So the year I didn't win, I was disappointed, but I tried hard to accept it.

Sometime during the year, I happened to read a published essay and realized that the girl who had won had passed off this author's work as her own. I was furious, filled with righteous indignation, and I wanted to go to the principal and tell him what I had discovered. But my mother wouldn't hear of it. She wouldn't let me do it. She told me the worst thing you could do in the Jewish religion was to embarrass someone; that this child had her own punishment having to live with what she had done. And though I resented it at the time, I went on to tell my children and now my grandchildren this story. I am so proud of my mother for seeing what really mattered—for helping me to understand which things in life are really important.

—Renee Burk, DAUGHTER, MOTHER, GRANDMOTHER

Mime Mom

If it had not been for my mother I doubt if I could have made a success of pantomime. She was one of the greatest pantomime artists I have ever seen. She would sit for hours at a window, looking down at the people on the street and illustrating with her hands, eyes, and facial expression just what was going on below. All the time, she would deliver a running fire of comment. And it was through

watching and listening to her that I learned not only how to express my emotions with my hands and face but also how to observe and study people.

It seems to me that my mother was the most splendid woman I ever knew . . . I have met a lot of people knocking around the world since, but I have never met a more thoroughly refined woman than my mother. If I have amounted to anything, it will be due to her.

—Charlie Chaplin,
PANTOMIME

Source: Alexandra Towle, *Mothers: A Celebration in Prose, Poetry, and Photographs of Mothers and Motherhood* (New York: The Watermark Press, 1988).

sometimes overlook the sweet moments in our everyday lives. Ellen Bialo's mom helped her to appreciate these times and taught her by example how to show kindness to others.

Lessons in Sweetness

When someone says to me "You're so sweet," or "You're so enthusiastic," or "You're so warm"—or whatever those things are—I think about how those are all the things I got from my mother. I never saw those things in her when I was a kid. I only saw her dependence and her difficulty in making decisions. But as an adult, I am able to understand who she was and realize what a wonderful role model she was and is for me. She taught me to be sweet to people, to listen to them—all those things you need to do to have relationships with people. It is because of her that I have good relationships today.

My dad died last year, and my mom, who's now eighty, just spent a week with me, and we had the most wonderful time.

We went to the theater and did things—girl things—that we just never found the time to do when my dad was alive.

Whenever I was sick and stayed home from school, my mom would play the music really loud and we would sing. During her recent visit, we sat around my living room, my mom nestled into my club chair, and we played CDs, listening to the music we played when I was a little girl. So *The Best of Kaylee Smith* was blasting through my speakers and we both started singing. And all of a sudden we were singing louder than Kaylee and we looked at each other and it was this moment from childhood—re-created right now. It was amazing. And I realized this is what I got from my mother—these amazingly wonderful moments that can only be experienced, not explained.

"... this is what I got from my mother—these amazingly wonderful moments that can only be experienced, not explained."

My mom and I also cooked together. She always did this thing—you know, a mom thing—where she would say, "You want to know how to make this?

You want me to write down the recipe? No, just watch me." So I'd watch her. She said the same thing last week as we stood in my tiny Manhattan kitchen, me wanting to learn how to make matzoh brie, and my eighty-year-old mother showing me exactly how to break the matzoh, just as she has always done, saying just what she always says, "If you don't break it this way, and you break it that way . . ." It was great. It was a moment I could have with no one but my mother.

—Ellen Bialo,

DESIGNER OF INTERACTIVE EDUCATIONAL SYSTEMS

Old Hickory Had a Mom

There never was a woman like her. She was gentle as a dove and brave as a lioness . . . The memory of my mother and her teachings were, after all, the only capital I had to start life with, and on that capital I have made my way.

—Andrew Jackson,
SEVENTH PRESIDENT OF THE UNITED STATES

Source: Lucy Mead, *Mothers Are Special* (New York: Gramercy Books, 2000).

difficult as it may be to allow their children to make mistakes, even moms know that sometimes experience is the best teacher. Sometimes children just have to learn the lesson for themselves.

No-Smoking Lesson

I had stolen a pack of cigarettes from the local drug store when I was in fifth grade. I closed the door to my bedroom, opened the window, sat on my bed, lit up, and blew the smoke through the window screen. At that time, I didn't know my mother had the nose of a bloodhound. (A few years later she smelled a leak in a gas line buried six feet underground.) Anyway, several hours after I finished my smoke, my mother walked past my bedroom. She did a double take and stuck her head back in. "You smoking in here?" she asked (not really asking). Being eleven, I was, of course, incredulous.

"Noo-wa."

She didn't even skip a beat. "Get your pack and meet me in my bathroom."

"Mom," I whined after her, "I don't even know what you're talking about." She was already moving down the hallway and didn't break stride.

"Just get your pack," she called. There wasn't a drip of uncertainty in her voice.

So I got my pack. She was sitting on a white wicker towel cabinet in the smallish bathroom off my parents' bedroom. She put the toilet seat down and motioned for me to sit on it. She handed me an ashtray and a book of matches. "Go ahead," she said. So I did. I lit up.

I was trying to cop that elusive adult coolness that comes from smoking a cigarette. It wasn't that I had any idea of who James Dean was at that time. But there I was, hunched over, my forearms pressed against my little fifth-grade thighs, the cigarette dangling from my overrelaxed, limp-wristed hand, squinting into the distance as I took each drag.

My mother sat there motionless, staring down at me. Not glaring. Staring. Not so much at me, as through me—without a trace of emotion. Her face was the picture of unimpressed neutrality. It got harder to stay cool. I started smoking faster to hurry up and finish the cigarette.

Once I had, my mother held out her hand for the dirty ashtray. I handed it to her. She reached down to open the lid of the toilet seat. I stood up. She dumped the dirty butt and ashes into the can, closed the lid, and cast her gut-wrenching emotionless gaze on me again: "You can smoke anytime you want. You just have to do it in front of me."

That was, literally, the last cigarette I ever had.

—Harry Gottlieb, INTERACTIVE DESIGNER/DIRECTOR

Our Moms Are the Best Nurturers Ever

Cold Compresses and Moral Values

Today, we think of nurturing as caring and feeding, and this, of course, is still the essence of what our moms mean to us. Despite the sexual revolution, it is still mostly moms, after all, who bake us pies, brush our hair, serve us cookies and milk, and call us in to the dinners they have made.

I remember a vacation long ago. I was twelve, standing at the door to my parents' hotel room at two A.M., knocking, saying, "Mommy, I don't feel well." She stayed up all night putting cold compresses on my forehead to bring down my 104-degree fever.

But, as the voices in this chapter tell us over and over, there is more to a mother's nurturing than chocolate chips and kisses on bruised knees. Over the years, my mom gave me an even deeper kind of nurturing when she taught by example that all people are equal, war is wrong, education is important, truth is essential.

Nurturing is not, at heart, the act of doling out material things. And our mothers, somehow, seem to understand this.

Raised

on positive energy, bad cooking, and a deluge of love notes, entertainment news anchor Laurin Sydney is the cohost of CNN's Showbiz Today, *television's most widely distributed entertainment news program. Laurin credits her mother with giving her the self-confidence she needed to make it this far.*

Wisdom in the Oddest Way

I think I am probably the most-loved person that I know.

I grew up thinking I could be the first female president if I wanted. I could grow up and be a TV anchor. I never thought there were any constraints on me because my mom gave me such a support system. My mom made me believe that if I put my mind to something and studied hard and took the steps to get there, I would. Of course. So I never knew there was a glass ceiling, or a men's club, because I was always taught: "Of course you can." And I was taught it in a very fun atmosphere—in a fun, supportive, spirited, energetic way. My mom's words of wisdom came out in the oddest way.

I had no aptitude for language. And I had to take French. I worked really hard, but I got a D. And since I did the best I could, my mom celebrated. She celebrated because I got a D in French. It's pretty darn wonderful for a parent to know that a kid is doing the best she possibly can. I never needed to have my head down for anything. I never was made to feel embarrassed. It was an amazing upbringing. My mom was so wonderful.

Kids would line up to have dinner at our house, just because sitting around our dining-room table was so much fun. And this was a woman who couldn't cook. Every night we'd have two dinners. One she would cook, and we'd move it around the plate, and then Dad would say, "Come on, let's go out for Chinese," and we'd have a second dinner. That's the only bad thing my mother ever gave me—my cellulite!

"I constantly got love notes from my mom."

I constantly got love notes from my mom. There's one on my bulletin board in my office. It's a heart and it says on the front, "Each year I think how much better I know you." Inside it says, "And love you." And then she wrote, "Every second, every minute, every hour, every week, every month and day after day, you are truly the most special daughter, friend. The world loves you and so do I—I'm the head of your fan club. Love always, Mom."

You know, the things my mom said, these things weren't pearls of wisdom. It wasn't knowledge that was passed on from one generation to the next—it was just this cushion of love that surrounded me. I'm so blessed and I feel it every single day.

—Laurin Sydney, CNN ENTERTAINMENT REPORTER AND ANCHOR

Mother Knows Best

The doctors told me I would never walk, but my mother told me I would—so I believed my mother.

—Wilma Rudolph,
U.S. Olympic gold medalist

Lynn

Huberman is Laurin Sydney's sister. She remembers their mom's unconditional love and their afternoon muffin tradition.

Muffins in the Afternoon

My mom, she's in my heart always. When she died, I read the line in *Tuesdays with Morrie:* "Death is the end of a life, but not a relationship." That's true for me with my mom.

I remember her unconditional love. I think about the times that she didn't agree with me but always supported me. I still feel and remember her smile and how that translated into a very warm feeling. I remember the excitement I would feel when I hadn't seen her in a while and was going to see her. Thinking about her now, I can feel the warmth again. My mom gave me that joy.

The special feeling I have from my mother's love for me made her the first person with whom I wanted to share any personal achievements, triumphs, or joys. I always felt that she, more than anyone else, could and would be the happiest person for me at special times in my life. Sharing my experiences with my mother doubled the joy I was feeling. It was an extra reward for me when I could feel how happy I made my mother from sharing my good news. Although she is no longer the first one with whom I am able to share good things, the relationship and her love for me is forever in my heart. I carry her love with me always and cherish how it feels.

"Sharing my experiences with my mother doubled the joy I was feeling."

Mom and I had a late afternoon ritual that started when I was young and continued almost until the end of her life. After we spent an afternoon together doing errands or shopping, we would wind up at a luncheonette or coffee shop for a pick-me-up. We would sit and discuss what we had just done, as well as whatever else needed to be discussed. I fondly remember those late afternoon chats over a toasted corn or English muffin. I remember them as being such special treats capping off busy days. To this day, if I'm out and able to stop, I do so for a muffin in the afternoon. It's a part of my mother that will always be with me.

My mom was beautiful—a very proud woman whose beauty was seen inside and out. She taught us how to care for ourselves and how to care for others. She was truly remarkable. I was and am so proud to have her as my mom—I just get that warm, fuzzy feeling when I think of her.

—Lynn Huberman, BOOK DEVELOPER

Safe in Her Arms

I can still feel my mother's arms around me, holding me, as she stood out on the porch and we watched a storm come rolling in across the lake, waves swelling, thunder crashing, lightning slicing the sky, and my mother telling me how beautiful it was. I found out later she was scared to death, but she taught me not to be afraid; I was safe in those arms.

—Betty Ford,
FORMER FIRST LADY

Source: Suzanne Beilenson, *Mothers & Daughters* (White Plains: Peter Pauper Press, 1998).

Teaching

a child right from wrong, nurturing its soul, is perhaps the most difficult yet important thing a mother must do. When she was a child, Barbara Stark found it difficult to understand and respect her mother's way of loving—as it turns out, of nurturing. But as an adult, Barbara was able to form a lasting bond of caring friendship with her.

True Love

As I look back, I realize it was my mother who always came through for me. When I was young, I felt we didn't understand each other all the time, and this was probably true, but we contributed a lot to each other and really, really loved one another. I am very lucky that I realized this before it was too late.

When I was nineteen, I ran away and eloped. When we came home, my mother and father had a wedding for us, but it was my mother who had told my father that that was the thing to do. She then had them furnish an apartment for us.

My mother had wonderful taste and a kind of daringness that I so admired. When I was fifteen, we went shopping for a dress for a college weekend. In those days everyone wore tulle, but I couldn't take my eyes off a white wool sheath that was covered in gold sequins. My mother, who was watching me stare at the dress, asked if I liked it, and when I said I thought it was "interesting," she urged me to try it on. Well, I did try it on, we bought it, and I was the only fifteen-year-old in white wool jersey with gold sequins!

"I loved her wonderful taste, her grace, her charm, and her humanity, and those are the things about myself that I like best."

I was impressed with my mother's generosity and her extreme grace. When we were growing up, she hired a man named Marshall to clean my father's dental office suite. It was a big job and my mother helped him. When World War II started, Marshall went off to war. When Marshall came home on a furlough, she asked him to dinner and sat him at the head of our table. It was the place of honor—something rarely done with "help" in those days. I was so impressed with her generosity. She was a very giving, loving woman whom I didn't understand as a youngster.

My mother was always looking out for me, like when she introduced me to my husband. I had been dating a man I didn't like, and I made the mistake of telling her this when she was visiting. Well, off she went on a shopping outing and when she returned, I said, "Don't tell me you found something?" And she answered, "Yes, and I gave him your phone number."

As I "thanked" her, I inquired, "How old is he?" and she said, "He's in his forties." I groaned, "Great, just like all my dates, another forty-year-old bachelor!" Well, we finally met, became engaged on our third date, and married in our third month. Early on in our relationship, my husband told me that when my mother had finished describing me to him, he was convinced I was the secretary general of the United Nations!

When I had my daughter Zoe, my mother was in Philadelphia and I was in New York. She made me promise to call her when I went to the hospital—when it was time—so she could come. So when my water broke, I called her and told her I'd let her know how it progressed and when to come.

There used to be a rule in hospitals that you could only see babies during visiting hours. I was having a very long labor, so I said to my husband, "You'd better call my mother and tell her not to come because she won't make it before visiting hours are over." And as I was finishing my sentence, a nurse came into the room and said, "Does anyone know an Ida Goldberg?" And I said, "Yes, that's my mother." The nurse said, "Well, she's down in the lobby." My mother told me later that she had said to herself, "I'm not waiting. My baby is having a baby. What am I doing in Philadelphia?" And she just came.

I once asked my mother, "What was the most important thing you ever did?" and she answered, spontaneously, "Loved my children." And I loved her. I loved her wonderful taste, her grace, her charm, and her humanity, and those are the things about myself that I like best.

—Barbara Stark, DAUGHTER, MOTHER, GRANDMOTHER

An Evening Comfort

I am sorry to say that Peter was not very well during the evening. His mother put him to bed, and made some chamomile tea; and she gave a dose of it to Peter.

—Beatrix Potter
The Tale of Peter Rabbit

Phyllis

George's mom had a profound influence on who she is and what she has achieved. She recalls growing up in Denton, Texas, and the ways in which her mom inspired her. As with many of the people who shared their stories for this book, she spoke of simple, everyday moments that had such lasting impact.

Miss America's Mom

I hope I'm half the mother to my daughter that my mother was to me. She never, ever pushed me. She would say, "Are you sure you want to do this?" or "Phyl, why do you drive yourself so hard?" She wasn't a stage mother. She was just "mother," something she did so effortlessly and lovingly.

My mother graduated from college at the age of eighteen—she was so brilliant she skipped three grades. She could have had an extraordinary career, but she was from a different generation of women—one that didn't offer the choices women have today. My brother and I were her accomplishments. We were what she lived for.

From the time I was born, she dressed me like a little doll.

She put little petticoats on me, which she starched herself. I always had white gloves on for church, as well as a hat, purse, anklets, and mary janes. My mother loved to sew for me, and all of my clothes were beautifully made.

I remember going with her to the fabric store in Denton, and we would look at the Simplicity and McCall's pattern books, and I would dream about the beautiful clothes. Mother would say, "I'll make that for you," and we would search together for the right fabric, the right trim, the right lining, the right buttons. She covered all my buttons! (It's enough for me to just sew on a button for my daughter or fix a hem. Who has the time?) Mother took great pride in all those things. When we came home from school, there were warm cookies and milk, butterscotch pies, coconut cream pies, chocolate pies. And if you asked her how she made them, she'd say, "Oh, you know, a little of this, a little of that."

> "I hope I'm half the mother to my daughter that my mother was to me."

Every night after I was cheerleading, or had gone on a date, I would go sit on the end of my parents' bed and talk to her. I'd tell her everything—I'd share things about my girlfriends, my boyfriends, my teachers. Whatever happened. She would listen intently and she hung on every word. My mother was my advisor, my sounding board. She let me go through my process, which I still have a tendency to do. She was always there for me.

She started me on the piano at the age of six with Dr. Isabelle Scionti, a world-famous concert pianist who had settled in Denton. My mother believed in me and put me with the best teacher even though she was very expensive. By the time I was eleven, Dr. Scionti felt I could become a child prodigy. I could compete in recording contests with people twice my age and win. My mother expected me to practice an hour or two a day, but her expectations of me weren't unreasonable. She just said, "Be responsible. I know you can do this." She would make me a beautiful dress for every one of my piano concerts, and when I walked onstage everyone would go, "Ahhhh."

Because I played the piano, it seemed like a natural fit when the local Jaycees, the chamber of commerce, asked me to enter the Miss Denton pageant. I could win scholarship money, which certainly would be very helpful for my family. So I entered, but I came in second. I had won it all—Miss Congeniality, swimsuit, evening gown, talent—but I didn't come in first place. It was an odd experience to win all that and not win. Tough as it was, I accepted it, and my parents were right there along with me.

"She has been my best friend through it all."

The following year the Miss Dallas officials called and asked me to enter, but I declined. And then they called my mother and said, "Mrs. George, would you please talk to Phyllis? This will be so great. She'll probably win the whole thing this year, and you have to think of the scholarship money." I told them no a dozen times. My parents told them no. It was a big N. O.

Well, at midnight on a Friday night just before the Miss Dallas pageant preliminaries, I walked in the door of my parents' house—home from college with an armful of dirty clothes, my dad asleep in front of the TV, and the phone ringing off the hook. I dropped my clothes in the foyer and ran to answer it. It was a pageant official, and for whatever reason—maybe catching me on the phone at 12:02—he talked me into entering the preliminary. If I had not answered the phone or brought my dirty laundry home or my dad had been awake, I never would have been Miss America.

Right away I called my mother, who was out playing bridge, and said, "Mom, I just talked to so-and-so from the Miss Dallas Pageant and told him I'd be there in the morning." The morning! She was great—very calm. She said, "Are you sure this is what you want to do, Phyl?" I told her I didn't know but that I had told him I'd be there. Well, she came home from bridge and went and found my old evening gown in storage. She dug out my old swimsuit, which was a doozy, and she found the shoes I had worn the year before.

My mother was right there for me. Her daughter had said she would do something, and my mother never questioned it. Although she probably thought I was crazy, she never second-guessed me. She knew that's how I would grow and learn. We were there the next morning and I got in the preliminary. I entered Miss Dallas and I barely won. From there I went on to Miss Texas—working my you-know-what off—and after that I became the 50th Miss America, the first one with a gold crown.

After I won, she and Daddy and my brother were right there on the stage with me, but then they whisked me off for interviews. When I got back to my room, I called my mother and we cried for about thirty minutes, because I wasn't going to see her for a long time. It was a very emotional moment.

It's hard for my mother to express her feelings, but I have always known what they are through her actions. She has been my best friend through it all.

—Phyllis George, FORMER MISS AMERICA, TELEVISION BROADCASTER, BUSINESSWOMAN

Reflected Glory

It was a memory that met us everywhere, for every person in town, from the highest to the lowest, seemed to have been so impressed by my mother's character and life that they constantly reflected some portion of it back on us.

—Harriet Beecher Stowe,
AMERICAN AUTHOR

Source: Alexandra Stoddard, *Mothers: A Celebration* (New York: William Morrow and Co., 1996).

mom often is the most influential person in her child's life. This is true for Jamie Pekarek, whose mom really taught her to look for the deeper meaning in life.

Only a Mother Would

How can I sum up my feelings for the woman who has been and will continue to be the most influential person in my life? I find words difficult but here are some of the reasons I love her so:

She held my hand when I needed it most, but let it go when it was time.

She helped me draw maps to my innermost dreams.

She gently or, when appropriate, strongly showed me right from wrong.

I grew up with no prejudices, but with an open mind and heart. She was the model for my humanity.

I stop and smell flowers, know how to appreciate a moment, to laugh and love and take time to stop and look at the stars to find the Big Dipper. She is a large part of my ability to embrace life and treat others with kindness.

She sees a child and nourishes the child's innocence, fragility, and innate goodness. She has passed along this tenderness to me.

She somehow managed to see me as not only her daughter but also as a strong, independent woman. We have successfully walked the delicate line between friendship and family. I have felt her equal in our place in mankind—this simple act helped develop my self-esteem.

I used to wonder why our souls were pulled together to go through our time on earth in such a warm, spiritual, loving dance. I don't wonder anymore—now I simply smile and enjoy the twirls, swirls, and occasional dips.

> "She held my hand when I needed it most."

I have a picture hanging in my room. It is of my mother and me. I was five years old. My mother was asked to teach CPR to the children, teachers, and parents at a social fair at my elementary school. To make it more engaging she asked me to help her. To make it fun she dressed us both up as clowns. Not only am I in two ponytails, but so is she. Not only do I have a silly clown costume on, but so does she. Not only do I look comical, but so does she. Below the picture is written: "Only a mother would."

Now I'm twenty-nine and I feel blessed every day.

—Jamie Pekarek, RECRUITING MANAGER AND GRAD STUDENT